Swing Trading:

The Ultimate Guide to Making Fast Money 1 Hour a Day

following work including specific information will be considered an illegal act irrespective of if it is done electronically or in print. This extends to creating a secondary or tertiary copy of the work or a recorded copy and is only allowed with an express written consent from the Publisher. All additional rights reserved.

The information in the following pages is broadly considered to be a truthful and accurate account of facts and as such any inattention, use or misuse of the information in question by the reader will render any resulting actions solely under their purview. There are no scenarios in which the publisher or the original author of this work can be, in any fashion, deemed liable for any hardship or damages that may befall them after undertaking information described herein.

Additionally, the information in the

following pages is intended only for informational purposes and should thus be thought of as universal. As befitting its nature, it is presented without assurance regarding its prolonged validity or interim quality. Trademarks are mentioned without written consent and can in no way be considered an endorsement from the trademark holder.

Table of Contents

Introduction

Congratulations on downloading '*Swing Trading: The Ultimate Guide to Making Fast Money 1 Hour a Day,*' and thank you for doing so.

The following chapters will discuss what swing trading on the market is and how you can get the most out of it by using the right strategies. When it comes to making a trade, there are a lot of things to consider and this book will help you get into details about every aspect needed to take conscious and smart decisions.

There are plenty of books on this subject on the market, so thanks again for choosing this one! Every effort was made to ensure it is full of as much useful information as possible, please enjoy!

Chapter 1: Understanding Swing Trading—the Differences Between Swing Trading, Day Trading, and Buy-and-Hold Investing

Have you ever heard the word 'swing trading' before? But have you ever understood what it really means? It's actually quite simple: it means making your money work while you do whatever it is that you want. Basically, it's a different way of thinking that you can use to make money. Growing up, most of us have been taught that we can only earn an income by finding a good job. And that's exactly what most of us do. But there is a big problem in this, if you want more money, you have to work longer hours. However, there is a limit to the number of hours a day we can work on, not to mention the fact that having a lot of money is somewhat meaningless if we do not have the time to enjoy it. This is why rich people do not have a job because they have the businesses that do the work for them.

Think about it, you have a job that allows you to earn over 2000 euros a month, but that takes you over 13 hours a day, 6 days out of 7, so about 11 remain and of course you need to take at least 7-8 hours of sleep (for a healthy lifestyle) then you need to consider the displacements and the time spent so you can reach work, you will only have 3-4 hours of free time remaining, most likely you will use 2 of those remaining free hours for dinner in the evening. In the end, you actually have 2 hours of free time per day. This is not enough for you to enjoy life to the fullest. You find yourself having a salary of 2000 euros a month (which nowadays is worth almost nothing with the increase in expenditures) that will just continue to accumulate and you absolutely won't have the time to enjoy them in any way as you will spend most of your waking hours trying to earn more. This is what most people would call the 'rat race.'

Is there a solution? Yes, it exists, and it is to take a part of your money and invest it properly in the financial markets, and letting it do the work for you. The possibilities are scary and risks are definitely involved but this can be extremely profitable. One example? Apple's stocks.

Apple stocks have risen at a frightening rate in the last 10 years, from $10 to about 100. This means that with an investment of only $ 1,000, you would now have over 10 thousand dollars. This is the power of online investments, it allows your money to grow in a completely automatic way.

Unfortunately, you can't do the same at work by having a duplicate finish your tasks, but instead, you can create an extension of yourself—that is your money—and put it to work. In this way, while you are busy burning away the hours at work, or while you are at the bar hanging out with friends, you can earn and make profits at the same time thanks to the investment you made. Put simply, you can expand your horizon through the effective application of your money and maximize your potential to earn even if you do not receive an increase in your pay, or even if you decide not to make an extraordinary one or if you are looking for a more beneficial job.

What is 'swing trading?' How does the

swing trading technique work? These are two of the questions that inexperienced traders can ask themselves. In fact, swing trading is, together with 'Day trading' and 'Buy and Hold trading,' one of the most commonly known ways to invest. This is why many traders pick this method to do their trading, it's already tried and proven. This manner of trade is the intermediate version between 'Buy and Hold' and 'Day Trading.'

Anyone who wants to try Forex trading, whether he is a novice trader or a market expert, must decide on which trading technique they'll want to use.

Swing trading is one of the most widespread and effective techniques, this trading method is also characterized by many aspects that facilitate its practice. So you can invest in this approach even if you do not have much experience.

The decision to follow the technique of swing trading, rather than another, precedes the actual operational phase and depends strictly on the preferences of the trader and the type of approach he or she wants to pursue.

To have a quick review of the basics, there are mainly three different trading techniques, as we have already mentioned. These types are classified on the basis of the reference time horizon:

- Intraday trading: open a position and close it within the day

- Swing trading: open a position and close it after a few or a few days

- Buy and hold trading: open a

position and close it after weeks or months

Swing trading is, therefore, the most flexible method of trading, which tries to balance the defects of other, more extreme methods. A method that takes the best of both worlds and tries to eliminate the greater problems which are found in the other methods.

After seeing what 'scalping is,' an extreme declination of intraday trading, we now understand exactly what are the advantages offered by the swing trading technique and begin to analyze its differences from the other main techniques.

Swing trading is an easy-to-learn trading technique that engages novice traders and more experienced traders, without taking up too much time or the fun hidden in trading. Swing trading, is in fact, that trading technique that allows you to open a position on Forex, short or long, and close it from there after a few days, capturing the sentiment of the change and the swing described in that situation.

The trend of a price follows the continuous swing, downward or upward, which may last one or more market days. There is, therefore, no fixed price, but your position adapts to price fluctuations. In fact, those who work with this method are really aiming for this price swing.

The swing trader is the one who identifies these oscillations and 'rides the wave' for a variable period of time, which is neither too short to limit the gains nor too long to risk the inversion. In other words, it takes advantage of the favorable trend of the moment for a short period of time, before moving on to the next opportunity of making a profit. Swing trading strategies can be carried out in a very different time frame, which can range from a few days to whole months. This will depend very much on the person's trading style since each one will opt for a different timing.

Forex is the ideal market to practice swing trading because primarily it is extremely fluid and full of traders. The result will be the description of trends with continuous oscillations, which will rely on the skill of the trader to fully grasp.

How do swing traders make decisions?

Technical analysis is important in forming a swing trading strategy because it is fundamental that you are able to identify the moment when a corrective movement can end and when you can trade in the direction of the prevailing trend, increasing the chances of achieving success. In conclusion, technical analysis can help you clearly identify entry levels.

Furthermore, many swing traders base their strategies on macroeconomic issues. This means that if, for example, a war in an oil-producing country breaks out, this increases the chances that the price of oil will increase. In this scenario, a trader could aim to go long on the oil, expecting that this event could affect market prices over the next two weeks. The identification of the topics is of great help in trading because very often the events that occur around us help us to evaluate the sentiment on the different financial markets.

Can I swing trade against the trend?

Some swing traders tend to trade against the trend but does this mean that their chances of making a profit are therefore lower? Not always, as an important part of swing trading is the 'multi-timeframe' analysis. This means that a trader does not analyze a single time frame on the graph but makes his decisions based on the analysis of multiple intervals.

As an example, suppose that the daily interval indicates an increasing trend. In contrast, the hourly and fifteen-minute intervals may indicate that a decrementing movement could begin in the short and medium term. In this case, the trader knows that even if the long-term trend is on the upside, he can still make profits in the short or medium term using the signals generated by the shorter time intervals.

Chapter 2: Pros and Cons — the Costs and Benefits of Swing Trading

How much should be traded today?

Another important point before starting the practice of swing trading is to understand how much you are willing to invest today. The amount of capital that you are willing to invest changes not only because of the trader's economic resources but also because of the degree of preparation.

For this reason, we consider it useful to advise you to start investing with a demo account, or a free trading account, which allows you to understand what the risks of online trading are, but above all to feel the trading strategies or even just gain additional knowledge while you practice with the trading platform. Given this, let's examine how much should be put in an investment today.

Swing trading capital today requires:

- The possibility of making use of its capital

- Use of financial resources in fruit-bearing operations

How much is the capital needed to start swing trading today?

There are many traders who associate the meaning of a large sum of money to the term 'capital.' Obviously, not everyone will agree on how much a capital should be exactly, but every trader decides to invest his capital, according to the possibilities or opportunities. So, for a basic level trader, investing €100 is equivalent to an experienced trader investing €1000.

Capital, therefore, is a relative amount for each of us. Almost always, however, capital, in its most general meaning, takes the form of a value that is very difficult to obtain and use for a possible investment.

Today we can tell you exactly how the world of online trading has become accessible to everyone, even to traders who do not have immense amounts of capital.

How much do you need to trade for tangible results?

There are brokers that offer the possibility of investing in the stock market even with only €100 of initial capital, a ridiculous amount, which allows you not only to experience the world of online investments but also to get rid of the baseless assumption that online trading or Stock exchange investments are only for those who own a lot of money. This is what I call a 'test capital.'

To understand this concept, we must consider it to be of fundamental importance; if one understands it, the very concept of capital takes on a different meaning; in fact, it will mean every definition of greatness or importance. In other words, the concept of capital will mean only the amount of money that is available and in the case of wrong investment does not affect the overall financial situation of the trader.

Be careful not to confuse this with the concept of carelessly investing money. In reverse! You will have to treat the money you plan to invest with the utmost respect and always keep its importance in mind. Just constantly remind yourself that you earned that money by working hard and you do not want to waste it.

Remember that investing in online trading is risky because of the possibility of losing the entire capital. So pay close attention to this concept. It does not matter what the amount to invest, or what capital is available! The important thing is to understand the value of the capital that you're planning to invest.

If you follow our advice, you can find out how easy and quick it is to do online trading or invest in the stock market with just a few steps, and especially like all of this today, is really affordable for everyone thanks to the internet. There is nothing left but to continue this path and make the information in this guide yours so you can learn how to invest today.

Understanding that investments must earn money for those who invest in them is a fundamental concept. Although it may seem rather trivial, not knowing where to invest is and above all, not the same idea. Understanding which sectors to bet on is not trivial!

There are 2 possible ways to invest money. Investing money also means making that money do the work for you and that is why you should invest money in the first place. In fact, we all know and understand that money is one of the major components of having a modern life. Money serves and is the basis of a myriad of fundamental activities that belong to our lives.

The 2 roads to follow are divided between:

- Having the money

- Using the money

To better explain these concepts, let's give an example. It is common for people to say: "Put the savings under the mattress." This concept, although quite trivial, teaches us this method that can make us owners of a certain sum of money in the future.

However, owning money does not require any investment. In order for money to bring great yields, it must be invested. The money must, therefore, be used, or invested, not just held. This is especially true when considering the constant loss of value cash undergoes every year because of inflation. Investing can be seen as a way to betting against money itself and this is what I tend to think about when considering an opportunity.

How can a capital be used to invest?

Various uses of money include shopping, buying consumer goods, a new smartphone, a new car, or even other consumer goods. But there is more to using money than fulfilling our basic needs or material wants.

Even having a small amount of money deposited in the bank or other fields, can't be considered wrong. In all these cases, money is invested and yields. This is the concept of using money to make more money and it is precisely the concept of investing today.

If you use the money as your investment funds it is quite certain it's being used to make more money. In this case, producing money does not require much effort and additional initiative on your part. We only have to hope that the markets we have invested in are always positive, that is, they always close with a gain for us. Of course, it does not mean that you can just forget about it, deciding where and how your money should be invest will always fall on to you.

To do this, you can rely on financial magnates or choose to invest in online trading or other markets thanks to online brokers, who can offer you a complete training on the markets and online trading, which will then allow you to invest your money and strategize accordingly to make the right choices.

By taking these training courses, you will be aware of some theoretical and technical factors. The more information you have, the greater the chances of earning for you.

Swing trading money today: 2 ways to swing trade

We can divide the investments into 2 big categories:

- Buy something, wait for its value to increase, and then resell it at a higher value so that you can make a decent profit. In this case, most investors buy and sell real estate.

- Investing by buying shares. In this case, the investor becomes the owner of a piece of the company for which he has taken out an action, with the hope that the value of the stock will rise so that he can then sell his stock to a new buyer or shareholder, and collect the profit.

At the moment, I will focus more on this last aspect, as I consider it the most developed and as this will certainly a greater and more diverse portfolio.

Investing in the stock market today is also possible thanks to 'options trading.' Basically, 'options trading' makes it possible to invest in shares and also earn from a decreased value. Buying this type of financial instrument, allows you to earn even if the overall value goes down.

Another widely used strategy to invest today and to capitalize on its capacity to lend money for a certain period of time and then receive it with interest. Today we will talk a lot about this sector and especially about bond investments.

What is the minimum capital that you need to swing trade?

This is one of the most recurring questions that are asked by people who would like to start and eventually dedicate themselves to this activity. The answer, as we shall see, depends on many factors and in this chapter I would like to clarify some aspects that affect the choice of initial capital.

Let's start immediately by saying that the amount we decide to allocate to the trading activity, whatever the objective we want to achieve, must not be a capital we need to supply our daily needs. It must be, as I like to call it, an 'available capital'.

In other words, since investing is a risky activity (and so it's trading), like any other financial transaction, the money we devote to trading if lost, must not, in any way, affect the status of our financial stability greatly.

The question we must ask is, if we lose the money we have decided to dedicate to investing, do we compromise our family's livelihood in any way? If yes, you can either reduce the amount up to the parameters of 'tranquillity' or avoid dedicating yourselves to this activity, at least until you are in a position to have a decent capital available that meets the minimum requirements.

Recently I happened to meet a gentleman who, wanting to follow my own course during a discounted 'launch' offer to start trading using my system, asked me if I could keep the offer for a few days, to give him time to release his savings invested in accumulation plans in his bank. Since those were his only (and small) savings, I calmly advised him to let go of the course and the real operation, at least for the moment, and in the meantime to focus on studying while waiting for better opportunities (read: pending to have an 'available capital.') This I think should be the philosophy of all those who want to devote to what is defined by many as one of the most beautiful professions one can dedicate themselves to.

After this first 'rock' we try to understand what is the minimum capital we should devote to trading. Which, as we said at the beginning, depends on many factors. Unfortunately, the current generation which was exposed to trading for the first is the result of misleading advertisements that exaggerated the achievement of incredible wealth or earning incredibly large sums from starting with just a few hundred euros.

Although it is true that with the advent of CFDs—which offer an excellent leverage on almost all financial instruments—and cryptocurrencies (which, in some cases like Ripple made over 16,000% in 2017) today it is possible to trade with just a few hundred euros, it is clear that we can't immediately become rich from investing a small amount of capital, or less likely, to have a lucrative extra monthly income.

Instead, we can reasonably think, so to speak, of 'biting ourselves' on real markets by acquiring the necessary experience. Only once we have obtained stable results, we will be able to use more capital and aim to have an extra monthly income to add to our income from work (which, in the meantime, I absolutely advise not to abandon).

So let's say we start to put stakes: if we have

an 'available capital' that is around €500, this amount can be enough to start if and only if, our goal is to check our ability to trade and to determine if we can achieve constantly positive results. In other words, it can be seen as a 'testing capital,' used to gather experience rather than profits.

But beware, we must not run the risk of using exaggerated leverage. This means that we will have to open up transactions (and CFDs give us this opportunity) with very small lots and be content with small gains (and have small losses). Otherwise, using maximum leverage, we would risk burning the amount instantly with just a very few transactions. If you want, you can go further into the topic in my article on leverage.

If the objective is to have an extra monthly income instead, then the amount that should be allocated to trading (and we always talk about 'available capital' in the indicated sense) must be at least 3,000 to 5,000 euros. Of course, the operation cannot always be dedicated to instruments such as CFDs because it would be unthinkable, with this amount capital, to operate on different instruments that require margins far higher than those required by CFDs.

With 3000 to 5000 euros—of course, once you have acquired the necessary experience and a reliable trading method— we can set ourselves the goal of having an extra income that is around 200 or 300 euros per month, maintaining a low-risk profile. They might seem a bit small and dissatisfying, but if we consider the percentage return on 'risk capital', it is a respectable ratio.

Advantages of swing trading

From all that has been said up until now, the advantages of this trading technique are clear. Operating through swing trading offers one the opportunity to manage their profits, with the aim of maximizing them over time without incurring risks of achieving unpleasant losses. Excellent in managing the stress, as it does not involve having to follow in a frantic and anxious manner unlike with intraday trading. The position is in fact held over several days and this 'spreads' anxiety in the right way.

Swing trading also allows you to settle. We have seen how those who work through buy and hold trading are likely to run into the situation of trying to widen their earning prospects as much as possible, given the few operations carried out. With swing trading, however, the goal is to focus on a part of the bullish or bearish movement, without having to buy on a minimum level or sell on a maximum level and thus, making a profit as a result.

Disadvantages of swing trading

But it is not all sunshine and roses. Like all things, this technique also has its disadvantages. In fact, this technique requires a fair study of the market and the meticulous creation of a strategy. Then, however, the losses are more consistent compared to day trading and generally turns out to be more boring because it is less adrenaline pumping than the other methods that take place all in one day.

How much can you earn?

The questions of people who aim to invest in stocks have always remained the same from the day the stock market was born and I would like to respond to these in depth. Example queries:

- How much do you earn in the stock market?

- How to start playing in the stock market?

- How do you earn on the Forum Exchange?

- How much can you earn by investing in the stock market?

- I lost everything in the bag

The last one will seem strange, but it is one

of the many searches that many users make. They are traders who lose their investment on the stock exchange and we should try not to make the same mistakes by studying the financial markets and investing with a non-high risk profile and a diversified portfolio.

An investor will always ask how much you earn by choosing to swing trade in the stock market and it's not quite easy to give this question a specific answer. Most professional traders, in fact, know perfectly well that the amount of gain that can be obtained on the stock exchange is also linked to subjective factors. It is these latter that really determine what is then called a 'gain.'

The return on an investment in the stock exchange is also linked to a series of elements restricted over time. Investing today on the stock market is certainly not the same way it was 10 years ago. In fact, back then, it was in full expansion. The FTSE MIB had reached very high levels and the performance of the individual shares seemed to increase continuously.

That era has been over officially for some time. Investing in the stock market today means exposing yourself to various risks that weren't present a decade ago. Entire sectors of the stock market, such as the banking sector, are not the only sectors subject to a seemingly unstoppable price erosion. This is another element to take into consideration when trying to understand how much you can earn on the stock market. Compared to the past, investing today in the stock market means being aware of the fact that there are securities whose relaunch still seems very far away.

All the factors listed belong to the determination of how much you earn with the stock exchange. It is a variable sum linked to contingencies. But is there a way to calculate when to invest in the stock exchange and when not to? In other words, is it possible to determine a minimum sum above which the investment was successful?

The minimum gain that can be obtained on the stock exchange and can be considered a successful investment is the result of a kind of summation. By removing the field from possible misunderstandings it is always important to highlight that the factors that need to be added do not concern the subjective sphere of the investor. Instead, these are purely objective elements.

The first, and most important, concerns inflation. When choosing to buy stocks, it is hoped that, at the end of the investment, the increased capital will not be lost with the increase in the consumer price index. Now it is clear that, when starting to invest in the stock market, the inflation rate is not known but only reputable. During the investment, however, we have all the information available to quantify what would have been the natural increase in the amount invested in light of the trend of inflation.

This makes it possible to get an accurate picture of the change in the consumer price index year after year.

Assuming that there are zero risk investments on the market (a postulate rather than a reality), investing in the stock market is worthwhile if the yield is higher than that which is obtainable with the risk-free security. To do this calculation you can take into consideration the government bonds of a highly developed country. The yields of these bonds, clearly low, must then be compared with those of the investment on the stock exchange.

The interest rate that is paid by this risk-free security must, therefore, be added to the index relating to the trend in consumer prices. Thus we obtain a first data which, however, is still incomplete. To determine exactly what is the expected gain of the investment on the stock exchange, a third element must be added. At this point, one enters the field of subjectivity. The third variable is an additional margin that compensates for the risk taken by the investor. Quantifying this third element is not at all simple. Traders, however, are used to quantifying the risk run in a couple of percentage points.

The definitive summation to determine how much you earn by choosing to invest in the stock market can be summarized as follows: inflation + return on capital + additional margin. In total, it's around 11 percentage points.

The 11 percentage points of return obtainable by investing in the stock market are gross. It is, therefore, necessary to subtract all the items of expenditure, including taxes. Furthermore, this is a level that is supported by a normal trend in the consumer price index. It is obvious, on the other hand, that today with low inflation, that minimum level tends to fall further. The summation alone, however, provides a partial picture of how much money should be earned 'at a minimum' on the stock exchange.

A very important factor is the duration of the investment. In this case, the rule is very clear: to obtain interesting returns, hold shares for very long periods. This happened over 10 years ago. In fact, at the time, economic growth seemed to be unlimited and the trend in inflation was positive too. In those years, the same stock indexes improved continuously. But that picture has failed today. Paradoxically, to make an earning on the stock exchange, based on the model mentioned, you would have to go back more than ten years.

All the major analysts say that investing today in the stock market makes sense only if the shares can be maintained for 10 years. It takes time to succeed, so, year after year, to accrue an interesting return. But over time it also serves a lot of confidence in a restart.

The example of banking sector securities is just the tip of an iceberg of what is happening on the stock exchange. If you look at the prices of the many stocks in recent years, you notice the total absence of lasting restart. It is true that this situation has been taking root especially in recent years, but who says that the picture will improve in a few years? This is the real breaking point compared to the past.

Today the balance of risks or opportunities hang, and not a little, on the first course. The factors to be taken into consideration are many starting from systemic risk. The stock market trend, in fact, has to deal with the macro framework of reference and it is pitiless. The global economic recovery, in fact, does not take off.

Going down to the domestic market, the underlying picture is even more deteriorated. For this reason alone, investing in Italian shares is already a less advantageous step than an investment in US equities. All reports of the International Monetary Fund do not leave much hope in this regard, the difficult situation is bound to last in the future. The overall risk is then increased as further elements of concern have been inserted into this framework. The examples, in this sense, are the Brexit but also the serious crisis faced by Italian banks.

Therefore, investing in long-term stocks remains a bet for strong hearts. The fact that the long-term risks have increased, however, does not mean that it is impossible to gain on the stock market today. There is a way to avoid being overwhelmed by these fears. The road is to focus on the short term. The means to travel this way is to rely on binary trading and Forex & CFD Trading.

Alongside the various factors that we have mentioned as elements of risk to be reckoned with by choosing to invest in the stock market today, there are also purely economic considerations that advise against the long term. That 11% we have indicated as the minimum sum that can be earned, in fact, is gross. In that percentage, in fact, various expenses are charged that derive from being a shareholder.

Those who choose to buy shares are subject to a series of taxes and are obliged to respect a lot of duties. It is obvious that if this happens at a time of financial expansion then it is not a problem. On the other hand, if it starts at a time of crisis, then it is a crucial factor that discourages the long term.

Investing today on the stock exchange means relying on 'Binary trading' and 'CFD trading.' In fact, only these two financial instruments make it possible to obtain a profit that is not subject to the many risks of the long term. With binary options and 'Contracts for Difference,' it is possible to bet on the progress of a stock even for very short time intervals.

This is especially true in the case of binary options. Investing in the stock market with options trading means betting on which direction that our action will take in the short time of 60 seconds following the opening of the trade. It is obvious that if the mechanism of operation of binary options is this, then all the talk about the risks of long-term investment makes no sense.

Options trading, on the other hand, is a

way to defend against the high uncertainty that is ultimately characterizing the markets.

These same considerations apply in the case of CFD trading. The latter very closely resembles the traditional purchase of shares. With CFD trading it is possible to buy instruments that are linked to the performance of specific actions. You earn and lose in relation to the trend of listing but with a substantial difference compared to the stock exchange.

In fact, when you buy CFD, you do not charge any duty. Also, the expenses of a commission are certainly not like those of the shares. Earnings, on the other hand, can be immediate. In this case, too, short-term investments can be carried out.

But where can you trade online today? In

recent years there has been a boom in authorized platforms. This covered both binary trading and CFD trading. The list below shows the best brokers to earn trading with the stock market. It is good to remember that the use of these instruments can lead to the loss of capital. For this reason, before betting on online trading, it is always better to practice on demo platforms. These allow simulating the trading activity without risking losses.

All the best trading platforms give this opportunity that can be exercised without time limits. By joining the practice on the trading platform and a study on technical analysis and fundamental analysis, it is possible to create a valid alternative to the investment on the stock exchange. How much you earn today with online trading is definitely higher than what you earn on the stock market. Testing with a demo account costs nothing. Today, however, the role of inflation has become secondary. The curve of consumer price trends leaves no room for misunderstanding. Inflation is increasing nowadays slowly and indeed, the risk of deflation hides around the corner. This is why we need to consider other elements to define and determine what we can earn today in the stock market.

Chapter 3: Risks and Common Mistakes to Avoid—the Specific Risks That Come With Swing Trading and How to Avoid Common Mistakes

The risks of swing trading regardless of the type of platform you'll choose can be divided into 3 different categories:

- Scam risk

- Risk on capital

- Psychological risk

For decades, the top experts in trading and then later on online trading, have become engrossed in these issues trying to find a solution to mitigate or eliminate the effects of risk on trading. Fortunately today we have reached excellent conclusions and great progress has been made in terms of prevention and management of all types of risk that are related to trading activity. If you also want to become a successful trader you need to know the risks of your professional activity to be able to take the necessary countermeasures.

Welcome to our guide, which you can use to pursue your career and earn well in the field of online trading. We now proceed by analyzing the type of risks and propose a possible solution.

Scam Risk

We can consider ourselves lucky because we write in a particularly quiet time regarding the scams in trading and more generally, online scams. For a long time now the network has spread widely on our territory as well as worldwide, so the authorities are organized to defend users of the internet and protect them from scams. In Italy, there is a very efficient postal police that regulates and enforces the law on most of the types of scams used on the network, while in the field of financial instruments and products in our country, CONSOB is particularly vigilant.

About ten years ago when this sector experienced its first real expansion, in fact, there were documented cases of scams of all kinds, there were even 'puppet sites' that were dismantled immediately after making fun of a few thousand users, robbing their deposits, but today, fortunately, the situation has radically changed, of course in a positive sense! Since online trading has become extremely popular and has become widespread, it's not an activity which can be abandoned and ignored, the authorities have taken the necessary steps towards establishing complete and total regulation today, an excellent result that secures all of the traders who make their investments online.

Council for the risk of fraud

This is the riskless 'heavy' because now it is very easy to avoid. It is sufficient to inquire well before registering and making a deposit, on the reliability of the broker. The names of the best brokers for online trading are known all too well and you will have no difficulty in finding them to immediately start on your trading activity protected by law, but also by the high-quality service that the best brokers today are able to offer: low minimum deposits, secure accounts, encrypted personal data, fast withdrawals and platforms with real-time data that cannot be tampered with. The risk of fraud is ultimately null if you choose official brokers and regulated by authorities such as CONSOB and CYSEC, in this case, there is absolutely no risk and you can operate in maximum safety

We talked about avoiding unreliable brokers without a CYSEC license. These platforms are a danger even if you actually made some money. In fact, there are sites that allow you to make deposits without problems in a few minutes by bank transfer or credit card. The bad surprise comes however when you want to withdraw your money. The operation will be hindered in every way, for example by asking for documents that cannot be provided or other devices to prevent profits from being taken home. If asked, the customer service will no longer be heard, the phone remains unanswered and the messages will be ignored. These are the signs of a typical scam. Unreliable payment processes are one of the most frequent fraud methods used by unreliable brokers.

Risk on Capital

Once you have deposited your capital with an authorized broker you must also avoid wasting it. Although online trading represents the business to be carried out on the net with the best prospects of absolute profit, about 80% of traders lose all their capital in a short amount of time. This happens because beginners underestimate the risk of loss and very often even those who already have a certain degree of experience do so.

Trading online means investing and an investment activity has two sides of the same coin. An investment can go wonderfully well, but it can also go terribly wrong. The traders, therefore, have the objective of making their income and expenses equally balanced, maximizing the opportunities for profit and limiting their losses as much as possible.

Losing is normal, there is no trader in the world who doesn't lose, even the best traders suffer losses from time to time, the important thing is that they are limited, contained and managed in the best possible ways. So no need for a hysterical crisis, dear trader, all you need is to be aware and operate the management of your capital wisely. Even if your losses are quite high, you can always recover thanks to the remaining capital, which however must now be invested with strict criteria in consideration to get the better of the adverse, poorly reasoned or unfortunate phases of your career.

Tips for managing capital risks

To teach capital risk management techniques you would have to write entire books on the subject, there are just so many tips and techniques at your disposal, so do not worry, all you have to do is inform yourself properly and you'll always see your capital grow and your balance of profits increase. To rationalize then act, this is the key to success in an activity like online trading, where not only do you gain but also exposes you to risks. Your trading must be planned with every possible detail in mind. You must look at your initial capital and divide it into a series of low-risk operations.

Imagine that the amount of your risk based on available capital is 100%, you must know that you have the freedom to break this amount and choose how much to risk for each trade based on the money you invest. If you commit your entire capital, which for example we will imagine amounting to € 1,000, in a single trading operation, in that case, your risk on the capital would be 100%! This means that if your operation goes wrong you will lose everything you have! At that point, it would be a very hard blow, but this does not have to happen and there is an obvious solution to the problem.

To avoid losing everything you have, you need to invest little or very little for every order you send to the market. You must never risk more than 2-5% of your total capital for each trade so at that point you can be sure that even if the operation goes horribly wrong, you have lost almost nothing, but if you have invested successfully you made a profit, that added to others can lead your account to increase significantly step by step consistently over time.

Psychological risk

Another very present risk, but also very underestimated by traders is the risk linked to the psychology of online trading. The risk in trading can in fact also arise from factors of emotional origin, a fact that too often we tend to forget and not calculate, but a microscopic error is actually committed. All the most experienced traders know how much the psychological factor counts in trading, it is so strong that it's even considered one of the main engines in the market.

Since you only represent a small cell in the great cauldron of the financial markets, the psychological risk is a purely individual fact but it must be dealt with effectively regardless. For example, very often it can happen if you suddenly make big gains by investing in online trading. You may think that this is good, but actually, it's bad. This great advantage often turns into a problem especially for traders without experience because it leads us to think that earnings are raining from the sky and are not the result of a reasoned and organized activity.

Council for psychological risk

A secret of professionals in the sector lies in knowing how to remain impassive and controlled in front of every event. The most experienced traders know how to remain impassive and stoic even in the face of unfortunate days with huge losses because they know that times will change and the chance for triumph will come.

The experienced trader will always remain absolutely calm even before big entrances because losing their calm or concentration will lead them to start thinking they're invincible and fully capable of dominating all the markets would be a very serious mistake that can result in impulsive and hasty decisions. If these are the effects on an experienced trader think about what happens to a beginner, a 'victim' of all these emotional upheavals related to the loss or to the earnings of money. The most important thing is to keep a cold state of mind and maintain a logical approach to everything.

Risk, as well as profit, is one of the essential aspects of online trading. Although it is a reality that must not be hidden and which cannot be avoided, every prudent trader has the possibility to manage it and adopt all the necessary countermeasures in order to obtain great profits and a sparkling success in this exciting activity. Managing risk is not impossible, you just have to learn how to do it. Once you learn how to choose a broker, how to manage capital, and how to control (and never repress) your emotions, all goals become attainable and real.

Chapter 4: Examples—a Few Brief Examples of How to Begin Swing Trading, As Well As Resources and Navigating Data

We have already spoken extensively about how to swing trade in the stock market and how this activity can generate very high profits. Precisely because of a large number of profits that can be obtained and this is also why many people aspire to become stock traders. But how do you learn to invest in the stock market?

The point is that the exchange is not a game. Every time someone uses the term 'play in the stock market' that means they're going down the wrong path because it is not a game, it is about investment. The best way to learn how to invest in the stock exchange is to start investing with an intuitive and easy-to-use broker. The best solution in my opinion? Definitely 24option. Among other things, those who register at 24option also get free excellent trading alerts to know where it's easier to invest in the stock markets.

Swing trading from home

The first characteristic of the swing trade in the stock market that is immediately noticed by the eye is that it is an investment that can be made directly from home. It is no longer necessary to go to the Bank to hand over the purchase orders to the employee on duty. Old traders feel nostalgic when they remember those bank branches that had become a bit of a meeting place for the 'Oxen Park,' given a large number of traders who met and exchanged information and observations. On one hand, it is a positive thing, since investing in the stock market through an Italian bank is the best way to get skim off commissions and even lose money, given the inadequacy of the tools offered.

The only positive aspect of these 'Oxen Park' meetings was the opportunity of passing on the necessary experience to people who were just starting to invest in the stock market. Learning to invest in the stock market guided by the comments and experiences of older, more experienced traders is something that is difficult to do if you work from home. To solve this problem you have the option to attend discussion forums and try to establish a dialogue with the most experienced users. Though, you must always be very careful in believing what you're told on these forums because not all the information gained is actually true.

Investing in the stock exchange from home, using tools such as binary options or contracts for difference, is much more convenient than going to a bank branch physically.

What are the best platforms to invest in if you want to trade from home? There are few platforms that are truly reliable and affordable. Among the best platforms to invest in the stock exchange, we can report are the following:

- Plus500: safe and reliable, it is a truly professional platform. Plus500 is a 'Contract for Difference (CFD)' trading platform that allows you to invest in thousands of shares listed on all major world markets.

- 24option: a truly safe and reliable binary options broker, perfect for investing in the stock market.

- IQ Option: one of the most innovative binary options brokers. It is very safe and reliable. Offers a free unlimited demo account in time and quantities. IQ Option is the only platform for trading on the stock market that allows you to start investing with just 10 euros.

How to start swing trading in the stock market

The first step to start investing in the stock market is to know what the stock exchange is. It might seem obvious but it's not like that. Many traders start stock trading without even knowing what it is. The stock exchange is the regulated financial market on which shares are exchanged, which represent securities owned by listed companies. Each share gives the right, as the case may be, to receive a dividend (a portion of the company profits that are redistributed) and to participate in the ordinary and extraordinary meetings of a company.

Usually, however, it is not advisable to invest in the stock market through the shares. The best way to start investing in the stock market is to focus on derivative contracts that have underlying shares. In this way, you get the advantage of increasing earnings and, above all, earning both when stocks go down and when they go up when you make the right prediction.

How to learn swing trading on the stock market

At this point, you are probably asking, "How can I learn to play the stock market?"

The title of this paragraph is a provocation because we know that we must not talk about gambling but about investing. In any case, how do you start? How do you learn? The best way to start is to have options. These derivative instruments, in fact, are very simple to use and understand. In fact, binary trading is very easy. If we choose a stock listed on a world exchange (one of the main ones, of course) we only have to indicate whether the price of the asset will be increased or decreased at the end of a period of time. It does not count the level of variation, only the sign counts and this is perfect for learning because the aspiring trader can concentrate only on a few fundamental factors, leaving out all the other unnecessary details. It must be said that options trading can produce profits so high that many traders are choosing to trade options only, although they do not need a simplified approach.

How to operate on the stock exchange

We have already seen that in order to operate on the stock exchange it is convenient to use derivative instruments, binary options are better to start with and, later, CFDs can also be adopted (Contracts for Difference).Another important choice to make when investing in the stock exchange, especially at the beginning, is to focus exclusively on the best stocks, i.e. those large, well-known companies listed on the world's major stock exchanges.

Among other things, the major options brokers and CFDs all provide access to the big stocks but not access to smaller listed companies, perhaps they can be found in secondary stock exchanges like the one in Milan. Though, these titles are usually an indicator of extreme danger and the novice trader who decides to choose them might be at serious risk of losing their hard-earned money.

How trades in the stock market work

For a wholesome level of information, I try to make a global overview of the functioning of investments on the stock exchange. In general, it is possible to invest in the stock market with the direct purchase of listed shares or with the purchase of derivatives. In general, for those who have the problem of how to start investing in the stock exchange, the recommended choice is that of derivatives, in particular, binary options. For those who want to buy the securities directly, the process is slightly more complex. You have to open an account for the custody of shares and on this deposit, you, unfortunately, pay a stamp. Moreover, this type of investment usually passes for Italian banks and involves high fees and poor service. Vice versa, for those who choose to invest in the stock market with binary options or CFDs, there are zero commissions and a service that really works very well.

Another way to invest on the stock exchange is through the use of mutual funds. Investments of this type work by purchasing a share of the fund. The managers then use the money obtained through the sale of shares to invest the stock exchanges. This is an indirect investment that delegates all responsibilities to fund managers. In some cases, decent profits can be made, but it has often happened that investment funds, especially if managed by Italian companies, have led to very terrible losses. Moreover, the tax treatment of this type of investment is incredibly penalizing.

Investment strategies

It is much better to do it yourself, then. But when you work with options or CFDs on the stock exchange you need to have investment strategies that you can rely on. In general, we can say that there are very simple strategies that allow us to predict the market trend based on the direct observation of the graphs. It is also possible to predict the market trend based on the news relating to the various listed companies. Finally, for those who wish to delegate the choice of strategies to others without incurring the costs of investment funds, it is always possible to subscribe to trading signals services. In practice, it is another trader (or group of traders) that indicates by e-mail, SMS or integration with the trading platform, what the right transaction is at the right time.

The investment in the medium and long-term is ideal for those who want to build a capital, or simply diversify and increase savings over time at reduced costs. Given their versatility, 'ETFs' can be used in different medium and long-term investment strategies, where they can support or replace traditional instruments, thus allowing the attainment of the set objective. Currently, the range of ETFs is so diverse that any FCI can be replicated (at a much higher cost).

A strategy to swing trade capital in the medium to long term is to resort to investment funds, which has seen a rise in popularity over the last twenty years. One of the main characteristics of the funds is that it allows the underwriter to enter the market with modest capital and to obtain professional management that will help them obtain positive results over time, with a moderate risk. Investment funds should favor more active management, even if this does not always happen. In addition to weighing on their final return, they are the highest management costs to which the same funds are subject, and whose impact is felt particularly in times of slowdown or stagnation of the market. In light of this situation, the investor could find that it is convenient to substitute the investment in funds with that of ETFs that aim to closely follow the evolution of its benchmark index while offering the maximum possible transparency.

In advance it cannot be said whether it is better to invest in funds or in ETF; to make this choice you have to decide if you want the manager to move away from the benchmark (and from which benchmark), this possibility is called 'active risk.' Active risk is not necessarily bad because there are some managers who are actually better than others, but in reality, they are few and are not always available but you can find them. If you decide to move away from the basic risk, you must be convinced that:

- Good managers exist

- That they are able to do better than their benchmark

- Above all, you must be capable of finding them!

If you were able to complete each of the three phases, it is appropriate to rely on active funds, otherwise, ETFs are preferred because they cost less and carry precisely where you decided to go, without additional surprises.

The techniques for choosing the ETF that best suits your investment strategies are different; an interesting methodology is applied to sector rotation is that the market as a whole is made up of different equity sectors, corresponding to the different economic sectors and their continuous alternation from the origin to the expansion and contraction phases. For this reason, the moments in which all the economic sectors grow or decrease simultaneously are quite rare.

The concept of sector rotation is useful in order to identify, on one hand, the stage of maturity of the current primary trend and on the other to select those sectors that are growing relative to their strength. For example, sectors sensitive to changes in interest rates tend to anticipate both the minimums and the maximums of the market, while the sectors sensitive to the demand for capital goods or raw materials generally tend to follow the overall trend of the market with delay. Through ETFs, it is possible to take an immediate position on a specific stock market, without necessarily being forced to buy the different securities belonging to that particular basket. In this way, it is possible to obtain an immediate exposure on this sector, at the same time benefiting from its growth in value, besides the advantages linked to the diversification.

For example, if one thinks that at a given moment the US market should grow in relative terms to a greater extent than the French one, it will be appropriate to make the first one and to underweight the second one. This decision can be reached by analyzing the comparative relative strength between the two markets, which compares two dimensions (composed of market, sector, securities or other indices) to show how these values are performing in a relative manner and their respect for each other. The trend changes expressed by relative strength generally tend to anticipate the actual ones of the financial activity to which it refers. It is, therefore, possible to use the relative strength in order to direct purchases towards ETFs that show a growing relative force.

The great flexibility of ETFs also allows the construction of a guaranteed capital investment; in times of financial turbulence, investors often turn to products that provide capital protection which is those provided by financial intermediaries that often have high fees and charges for customers. Not many people know that it is possible to build a guaranteed capital product by yourself, which respects your personal investment needs! The central point of the logic of guaranteed capital is interest rates and the duration of the investment because at the base of all there are the two central concepts of finance:

- The higher the interest rates, the greater the return on the money

- As the duration increases, you earn more, because money 'works' longer

The money we will obtain in many years can be brought to today, as for bills that follow the discount law (the technical term of bringing the future money to today). You can easily answer the question: "To have 100 euros in seven years, knowing that the rates are at 5%, how much money do I have to invest?" This statement indicates how much money is needed to invest today to get the desired amount at maturity. The bonds that only allow the fruits to reach maturity, without paying interest during their life, are called zero-coupon bonds (ZCB) and are quite common on the market. If for example I want to have € 100 at maturity and interest rates are at 5% I will have to invest in zero coupon bonds € 95.24 (if the deadline is between 1 year) € 78.35 (if the deadline is in 5 years) € 61.39 (if the deadline is 10 years) 48.1 € (if the deadline is between 15 years) and 23.21 € (if the deadline is 30 years)

In effect, by building an investment with guaranteed capital, one only has to decide how to invest the remaining part of the initial 100 euros that have not been allocated in the zero coupons. An ideal solution is to invest in options because, thanks to the leverage effect, they can amplify any yield. If you have an investment profile that's less than aggressive, ETFs are excellent tools to build a guaranteed capital investment. If, for example, we assume a 10-year investment with rates of 2.5% for that maturity, the portion to be invested in ZCB is equal to 78.12%, while the remaining 21.88% will be invested in ETF.

This investment strategy makes it possible to achieve a minimum (not real) 'money' return target with few operations, as the ZCB provides for the repayment only on the nominal amount of the loan (not discounted with the inflation rate). It is, therefore, a valid methodology for those who intend to make investments with clear objectives and have little time to devote to monitoring the values as only an operation until expiration is deemed necessary. Unlike a guaranteed capital product offered by any financial intermediary, an investment of this kind built independently with ETFs can be dismantled entirely or in pieces (selling only the ZCB or active assets, ETF) to meet any need. Naturally, only at maturity will there be a certainty of the pre-established return and, over the course of the loan, a temporary adverse trend in financial variables, (rates rise by lowering the ZCB and at the same time decreasing the value of the ETF) could result in the liquidation of losing positions. The same consequence would be selling a structured bond, with the advantage that 'doing it at home' the commissions are much lower and you can separate the two components and, if necessary, liquidate only one, according to your specific needs.

Conclusion

Thank you for making it through to the end of '*Swing Trading*: *The Ultimate Guide to Making Fast Money 1 Hour a Day,'* let's hope it was informative and that it was able to provide you with all of the tools you need to achieve your goals whatever they may be.

The next step is to start applying what you have learned during the course of this book and get started right away. Our suggestion is always to open up a demo account and make a few tries, before putting real money into it. Remember that you should never risk more than what you can afford to lose, so manage your capital wisely.

Finally, if you found this book useful in any way, a review is always appreciated!

Description

Are you looking for a great book about swing trading in the stock market but every single time you purchase a course it seems that nothing makes sense? Are you scared when you hear words like 'capital,' 'online trading,' and 'stock?'

Then this is the right book for you! In *'Swing Trading: The Ultimate Guide to Making Fast Money 1 Hour a Day,'* you are going to learn everything there is to know about this topic and get insightful lessons that will transform your mindset when it comes to money.

In this in-depth manual, you are going to learn about fundamental topics such as:

- **What initial capital is required to start swing trading, so that you know if you have the right** credentials to get started in this amazing world or if it is time to save money before going on the attack

- What are the pros and cons associated with swing trading?

- Beginner friendly strategies ready to use today to increase your revenue and limit losses

- A detailed description of the most important strategies that will allow you to predict market's movements accurately and making the most out of them

- The difference between swing trading, day trading, and buy and hold

- **A lot of hidden information that will boost your education and get you started investing as fast as possible**

As you can see, this book is full of details and goes very deep on the subject. Prior experience is not required and the manual was written especially for those who do not know anything about swing trading.

If you have been on the fence for a while and want to take your swing trading game to the next level, this is the right book for you. Get it now at a special price and act fast—it won't be so cheap forever.

www.ingramcontent.com/pod-product-compliance
Lightning Source LLC
Chambersburg PA
CBHW071502210326
41597CB00018B/2658